D0909075

Schweitzer at work on the Goethe Oration, 1932

THE PATH
TO RECONSTRUCTION

A Brief Introduction to
Albert Schweitzer's
Philosophy of Civilization

BY

MRS. CHARLES E. B. RUSSELL

Author of
"General Rigby, Zanzibar, and the Slave Trade,"
"My Monkey Friends," etc.

WITH THREE PHOTOGRAPHS
BY THE AUTHOR

NEW YORK
HENRY HOLT AND COMPANY

MADE IN GREAT BRITAIN
PRINTED BY R. & R. CLARK, LIMITED, EDINBURGH

Contents

Illustrations

by the Author

Note

FOR those who are totally unacquainted with the German language, it may make what follows easier to grasp if I explain a few of the expressions which Dr. Schweitzer frequently uses, expressions which, familiar and simple in the original—for he avoids the technical phrases of the philosophers—have in English no exact equivalent.

WELTANSCHAUUNG. Many writers, for want of an English word that conveys exactly the same very wide meaning, use the German word to express what it stands for. But to the general reader unfamiliar with a foreign language nothing is more annoying than to be constantly encountering a word he cannot even pronounce. Dr. Schweitzer himself defines "Weltanschauung" as the sum-total of the thoughts which the community or the individual think about the nature and purpose of the universe and about the place and destiny of mankind within the world. I therefore propose to give it an English form by using the terms "world-view", "outlook on life", "philosophy", as may best suit the context. It should be noted that the one German word "Welt" does duty for our two words, universe and world.

GEIST and GEISTIG. Here again the Germans have only one

word where we have two. We say mind and spirit, mental and spiritual, where they say only spirit and spiritual. I shall translate always by using the latter terms, comprising both senses in the one word, but it must be remembered that the meaning is wider than that we often attach to spiritual, and the word may therefore sometimes appear not quite appropriate.

WORLD- AND LIFE-AFFIRMATION. This means that man has an inner conviction that life is a real thing, that the world in itself and life in itself have great value, that life is for each individual infinitely worth while, that the human spirit can dominate nature, and that man must never admit defeatism. It is the characteristic European attitude to human life.

WORLD- AND LIFE-NEGATION is the contrary belief, that life is an illusion, that nothing really matters because all is vanity, that the individual in his short span of life can achieve nothing of value, that the supreme good is to make an end of it. This is the characteristic Indian attitude to life.

CIVILIZATION. The exceptionally wide and comprehensive meaning attached to this word should also be kept in mind throughout. Dr. Schweitzer defines it as the sum-total of all progress made by mankind in every sphere of action and from every point of view, in so far as this progress is serviceable for the spiritual perfecting of the individual. Its essential element is, he says, the ethical perfecting of the individual and of the community.

REVERENCE FOR LIFE. This phrase too is immensely wide in its meaning, embracing as it does the whole span and the whole scale, in all its degrees, of a single and constant attitude towards all life as such, including even those forms of life which are injurious to our lives.

Professor J. A. Cramb, author of *The Origins and Destiny of Imperial Britain* and *Germany and England*, came very near to Dr. Schweitzer's teaching of reverence for life as the foundation of civilization when he said, in a lecture at Queen's College, Harley Street, some forty years ago, that the only standard by which we can measure civilization is the value it places on human life. Schweitzer goes further, as will be seen, in that he omits the word "human".

Preface

AT an early stage of our friendship, I was once with Dr. Schweitzer when, with a view to a possible future recital, he was trying a cathedral organ. It was at Ulm, on his way home to Alsace after receiving an Honorary Doctorate at Prague. His method is to play the same passage, generally of a Bach Prelude or Fugue, several times with different stops in order to discover which are the best for that particular passage on that particular organ. He asked me to go down to the nave, and then come up and tell him each time how the organ sounded down there far below. "But," I protested, "though I love it, I know nothing whatever about music! I can't play a note." "That's just why your judgment will be of value," he replied. "You will be able to tell me whether it will sound beautiful to the ears of the ordinary people in the audience, without your mind being distracted by all sorts of technical considerations."

My position is the same with regard to philosophy. I feel absolutely unequipped for the task I have been requested to undertake, and no one could be more delighted than I should be, if some scholar versed in the subject would relieve me. I am just one of the ordinary people in the world's audience, but in this capacity I do feel strongly that Dr. Schweitzer's is exactly the philosophy for which this distressful age is waiting—a philosophy within the reach of all, a philosophy which allows absolutely no barriers between man and man, the philosophy of reverence for life, the Christian thought in simple philosophic terms, of which one chapter is written in action in the hospital on the banks of the Ogowe River, of which, after himself superintending the clearance of the jungle, he was not only surgeon and physician, but architect, master-builder, carpenter and house-painter largely with his own hands. For though he holds four doctor's degrees—in music, medicine, philosophy and theology—earned at his own University of Strasbourg, and many others bestowed elsewhere *honoris causa*,[1] he regards no labour, however tedious or unpleasant, as beneath him.

It is noteworthy that to Goethe in his old age land reclamation and surgery were the conclusion of the whole matter for the two great creations of his imagination, Faust and Wilhelm Meister, and that these are among the things which Schweitzer has taken in his stride.

I myself discovered Schweitzer and was led to his books, and from his books to helping him in Africa, by a chance reading of a short but admirable article in the *Hibbert Journal* entitled "Schweitzer's Ethic" (July 1925). That experience makes me feel that my present task of attempting a simple introduction to his philosophy is better ill done than not done at all; and gives me hope that this inadequate little book will prepare the way in some minds

[1] Philosophy at Prague and Zürich, Divinity at Oxford and Edinburgh, Music at Edinburgh, Laws at St. Andrews.

for a study of the Doctor's whole work. From his childhood on, his thought and work and life form a remarkable
unity, and no one can really understand and appreciate
even the hospital in which so many English-speaking
people take an interest without reading his books, especially the two concerned with his Autobiography[1] and the
two volumes so far published of his *Philosophy of Civilization*. But I would urge my younger readers, if possible, to

[1] *Memoirs of Childhood and Youth*, 1924; *My Life and Thought*, 1931.

Of these E. Stuart Bates, in his comprehensive two-volume work
Inside Out—An Introduction to Autobiography (B. Blackwell, Oxford,
1936-1937), says:

". . . Side by side with any autobiography, read Albert Schweitzer's
Memories of Childhood, and the qualities and defects of the other will
straightway stand out in relief" (vol. i, p. 11).

"It can only be in the distant future that the value of his work at
Lambaréné can be estimated, if ever; but it is clear already that few
men, in any century, can have had so much to show in return for a
lifetime as he has done there. In addition, his work either as theologian,
or as musician, or as organist and organ-expert, constitutes a sound
and satisfactory life-work in itself. And the influence of his personality
and methods makes itself felt beyond the limits of any section of his
work, epitomized as they are in this record of his own, itself an
epitome of all the uses of Autobiography" (vol. ii, p. 61).

"Nothing has been said about the Hospital work. Little is said in
the book. The main thing is that each interest, as it emerges and leads
on to a conclusion based on study, and directs itself towards some
practical end, either in action or enlightenment, contributes towards
creating Autobiography in its most fruitful form. Thought and
meditation, narrative and progress are exhibited in interdependence.
No better example of a human being at work; the whole organism bit
by bit unfolding and building itself up step by step, finding and
creating its own mission and fulfilment, always getting something
done and making each new something the basis of further development; finding contentment in its own activities, stimulant in its own
vitality and perceptions, reward in its own consciousness, hope and
faith for the future in the recollection of the past and the call of the
present" (vol. ii, pp. 65, 66).

learn German, for Schweitzer's writing, like Goethe's, does not translate well into English, and just as it is well worth while to learn German to read Goethe alone, so it is to read Schweitzer alone. To take but one point: the extraordinary wealth of metaphor drawn from nature employed by both cannot in translation be reproduced in all its charm. What Schweitzer says of Goethe in this regard might well be said of his own writings:

"How beautiful are his metaphors! He does not invent imagery to fit a thought, but the pictures of what he has seen and experienced, stored in his mind, wait within him ready for the thought which is destined to gain form from them" (*Goetherede*, p. 16).

Schweitzer's metaphors adorn nearly every page, and in some passages his German prose reaches a height of great poetic beauty. Examples of his metaphors will be found in Chapters II and III, and here, comparing two of Bach's Sonatas, is another:

"As one listens (to the first) one feels one is strolling along the banks of a woodland stream or over meadows sown with diamonds by the morning dew. The latter work transports the hearer into high alpine regions where vegetation ceases and the mountain peaks, towering behind each other, stand in sharp outline against the azure sky" (*J. S. Bach*, p. 391 in the original).[1]

While I set about my enterprise with deference and

---

[1] Cf. "Es gibt wenige philosophische Schriftsteller, deren Werke eine ähnliche Fülle treffender Vergleiche enthalten wie die Arbeiten Schweitzers" ("There are few philosophical writers whose works contain such a wealth of apt metaphor as the works of Schweitzer") (*Albert Schweitzer, sein Werk und seine Weltanschauung*. Oskar Kraus, 1929).

humility and much misgiving, I am encouraged by re-
membering an episode narrated by Dr. Schweitzer in *My
Life and Thought*. It occurred when, as an Alsatian, he had
been brought back from French Equatorial Africa as a
prisoner of war and was an internee at the camp of
Garaison in the Pyrenees. Let me quote it in full:

"Not long after our arrival some new-comers arrived
from another camp which had been broken up. They at
once began to grumble about the bad way in which the
food was prepared and to reproach their fellow-prisoners
who occupied the much-envied posts in the kitchen with
not being fit for their job. Great indignation thereat among
these, who were cooks by profession and had found their
way to Garaison from the kitchens of the first-class hotels
and restaurants of Paris! The matter came before the
Governor, and when he asked the rebels which of them
were cooks, it turned out that there was not a single cook
among them. Their leader was a shoemaker, and the
others had such trades as tailoring, hat-making, basket-
weaving, or brush-making. In their previous camp, however, they had applied themselves to do the cooking, and
declared that they had mastered the art of preparing food
in large quantities so that it was just as tasty as when prepared in small quantities. With Solomon-like wisdom the
Governor decided that they should take over the kitchen
for a fortnight as an experiment. If they did better than
the others, they should keep the posts. Otherwise they
would be put under lock and key as disturbers of the
peace. On the very first day they proved with potatoes
and cabbage that they had not claimed too much, and
every succeeding day was a new triumph. So the non-
cooks were created "cooks", and the professional cooks

were turned out of the kitchen. When I asked the shoe-maker what was the secret of their success, he replied: 'One must know all sorts of things, but the most import-ant is to do the cooking with love and care'." [1]

[1] The passage concludes : " So now, if I learn that once more someone has been appointed Minister of some department about the work of which he knows nothing, I do not get as excited over it as I used to, but screw myself up to the hope that he will prove just as fit for his job as the Garaison shoemaker proved to be for his".

THE PATH TO RECONSTRUCTION

CHAPTER I

Introductory

WHAT is philosophy? The love of wisdom. And wisdom is what men should live by and what all men who think at all do love. But philosophers have strayed so far from the original simple meaning of the word that now for the masses it means something almost to be afraid of, or to be shunned as being something necessarily abstruse, some profound, unintelligible process or system of thought wrapped up in incomprehensible technical jargon[1] and far remote from any application to their own lives. Thus have philosophers done great wrong to their fellow-creatures, who are constantly thirsting for intelligible yet sound guidance, and thirsting so eagerly that for lack of it they are ready to gulp down any idiocy, *e.g.* Nazism, if only it be set before them clearly and definitely.

Dr. Schweitzer urges us all to become thinking individuals, telling us that if men would but meditate even only a little on the infinite and the finite, on the meaning of

[1] "Technical expressions are a danger for every system of philosophy. . . . For they may become formulae which hinder the natural development of thought in the same way as ruts in a road hinder traffic" (Schweitzer, *Indian Thought and its Development*, p. ix).

life and death, then the foolish, passionate ideals of the men who often make public opinion would have no more influence. He is confident that by the path of thought, if we will but enter it and follow it with fearless faith in truth, we can find salvation.

It seems indeed, he says, writing in the years preceding 1923, like mockery to urge men to reflect on the meaning of life at a time when unemployment and poverty and hunger are rife, and when power is being exercised by the strong over the weak in the most shameless and senseless fashion. Yet nothing but a revival of thought among the peoples can put an end to all the chaos and misery around us.

The reawakening of the spirit then must begin with a realization by educated and uneducated people alike of their lack of a sound philosophy or world-view, and with a realization of the horror of this unthinking condition. The power and the right to think individually is part of man's birthright, the hall-mark of human nature, yet it is weakly surrendered, often without the potential existence of such a power and such a right even having been realized. Dr. Schweitzer hates the herd-life we lead, wanting to do everything in groups and societies and committees and nations and churches, instead of directly seeking the right as individuals and facing our individual responsibilities.

Previous European writers on philosophy have tried to explain our life as part of the universe, or to explain the universe and fit us into it. Schweitzer boldly and unreservedly asserts that we can never hope to explain the universe, the world, in which are manifested such mysterious, inexplicable contradictions. But, he says, we need not fear that without understanding of the universe everything in our thought will fall into ruin. By no means. We must be content to learn what we can about ourselves—and be content with the fact that we cannot reconcile the God we see manifested in the world, with its pitiless waste and cruelty, with the God manifested in the heart of man in infinite love and pity. Why concern ourselves with our relation to the universe? If each one of us becomes a thinking being in the full sense of the word "thinking", which involves heart as well as head, he cannot fail to get into relationship with the Eternal, and that is what really matters. Thinking, carried far enough, always reaches a point where mysticism begins.

The basic principle of Schweitzer's philosophy is that if we think about life, we shall arrive at one certainty that is indisputable, based on this as a foundation for our whole outlook on life—that in ourselves and in all that has life there is will-to-live, a universal shrinking from annihilation and from the depreciated will-to-live which is pain, a universal desire for the enhanced will-to-live which is pleasure.

Whereas other Western philosophers have shut out animals from their scheme of life, Schweitzer says that every form of life is a manifestation of the one, infinite, inscrutable, universal Will, and that our guiding principle, not only towards human beings, but towards everything that has life, should be reverence for that life, which is the same divine mysterious force whether in man or dog, or flower or flea. Therefore we must not do anything prejudicial to any form of life without first asking whether our action is necessary. We are obliged to destroy and damage some life in self-defence and some life in order to get our food, but we ought never to be complacent but always scrupulous and regretful about it, we ought never to cause any death or any suffering beyond what we absolutely must cause, and we ought to try to make up to other living creatures for the harm we have to do to some of them. Thus because our feet may maim countless insects as we walk, we are under an obligation to stoop to move from the path the worm we do notice in passing which might be crushed by the next comer. This is not a triviality, but an example in miniature of a basic and universal moral principle. It is precisely because the black man suffers terribly from the white having taken possession of his country, because of the frightful history of the slave trade in the past, and the multiform exploitation in the present, because of the drink which has poisoned him, because of the horrible diseases before unknown to him which have been introduced, because he has been robbed of his land and is treated with harshness and contumely and so on—it is because of these things that it is an imperative moral duty to sacrifice ourselves to make reparation and bring him relief.

What then is the rule of life for the man who would obey the law of ethics? He must himself, as far as he can, help and further the universal will-to-live in all its manifestations, and he must himself make such reparation as he can to those in whom life has been thwarted and crushed. He must dedicate his life to the suffering life that most needs it, he must take on himself the sins and responsibilities of his fellows, he must accept boundless responsibility

4

Reverence for Life: Dr. Schweitzer with a patient, 1927

Reverence for Life : An orphan, 1938

and act up to it. Schweitzer has written "Christianity, as the most profound religion, is to me at the same time the most profound philosophy"[1], and surely we have here, translated into terms of practical philosophy, the Christian teaching to take up the cross. But most of us interpret that Christian teaching as meaning that we are to bear patiently and as cheerfully as we can the cross that *comes* to us. Dr. Schweitzer seems to say that we are to *seek* our cross, and so he teaches by his own example.

Reverence for life, the idea once grasped, can never be forgotten. For it is an idea that clings. It is a great driving force that kills complacency. It allows its disciples no rest. But it makes all life fuller and more interesting, and brings its great reward in deepened realization of what a mysterious, universal, glorious thing life is. It is an idea that may be applied to every human relationship. Possessed by it, we shall respect the personality of those we think the lowest in the human scale; we cannot quarrel or condemn another. And of course we cannot perpetrate, or allow to be perpetrated, so many useless, unnecessary cruelties upon animals.

Reverence for life is of course no new idea. We find it for example in many of our English poets.[2] But the phrase, only formulated by Schweitzer long after the idea had begun to rule his life and had driven him to Africa, gives

[1] *Christianity and the Religions of the World*, p. 83. But he expressly disclaims for Christianity, in comparison with other faiths, any pre-eminence that cannot be maintained by thinking and by the intrinsic truth for which it stands.

[2] In Cowper, Wordsworth, Tennyson, Coleridge, Longfellow for example, who all wrote under the influence of the Rationalism which Schweitzer finds so admirable.

fresh cogency and fresh comprehensiveness to the idea it stands for. As do the facts of his life, for did ever man make a greater sacrifice than, under the compulsion of this idea, he has made? In British newspaper and magazine articles I have often found him mentioned along with Livingstone and Grenfell. But without any disparagement of those two great heroes, it may be said that the comparison misses one vital distinguishing point. For what was Livingstone before he went to Africa, and who was Grenfell before he went to Labrador? Whereas Schweitzer was already a very famous man in academic circles, in philosophy and theology as well as in music, when he abandoned a conspicuously successful career and everything that he loved by going to a pestilent spot on the Equator as a mere medical missionary.

As we may learn from his *Memoirs of Childhood and Youth*, he had really been possessed by the spirit of this principle of reverence for life from his earliest years. As an infant not yet attending school, he repeated secretly every night a prayer he had composed asking God to bless everything that has breath. And he tells us that the two great experiences of his youth were the following:

"A deep impression was made on me by something which happened during my seventh or eighth year. Henry Brasch and I had made ourselves catapults, with which we could shoot small stones. It was spring and the end of Lent, when one Sunday morning Henry said to me, 'Come along, let's go on to the Rehberg and shoot some birds'. This was to me a terrible proposal, but I did not venture to refuse for fear he should laugh at me. We got close to a tree which was still without any leaves, and on

6

which the birds were singing beautifully to greet the morning, without showing the least fear of us. Then stooping like a Red Indian hunter, my companion put a pebble in the leather of his catapult and took aim. In obedience to his nod of command, I did the same, though with terrible twinges of conscience, vowing to myself that I would shoot directly he did. At that very moment the church bells began to ring, mingling their music with the songs of the birds and the sunshine. It was the warning-bell, which began half an hour before the regular peal-ringing, and for me it was a voice from heaven. I shooed the birds away, so that they flew where they were safe from my companion's catapult, and then I fled home. And ever since then, when the Passiontide bells ring out to the leafless trees and the sunshine, I reflect with a rush of grateful emotion how on that day their music drove deep into my heart the commandment: 'Thou shalt not kill'.

"From that day onward I took courage to emancipate myself from the fear of man, and whenever my inner convictions were at stake I let other people's opinions weigh less with me than they had previously. I tried also to unlearn my former dread of being laughed at by my schoolfellows. This early influence upon me of the commandment not to kill or to torture other creatures is the great experience of my childhood and youth. By the side of that all others are insignificant."[1]

"The thought that I had been granted such a specially happy youth was ever in my mind; I felt it even as something oppressive, and ever more clearly there presented itself to me the question whether this happiness was a thing that I might accept as a matter of course. Here then was the second great experience of my life, viz. this

[1] *Memoirs of Childhood and Youth*, pp. 40-42.

question about the right to happiness. As an experience it joined itself to that other one which has accompanied me from my childhood up; I mean my deep sympathy with the pain which prevails in the world around us. These two experiences slowly melted into one another, and thence came definiteness to my interpretation of life as a whole, and a decision as to the future of my own life in particular.

"It became steadily clearer to me that I had not the inward right to take as a matter of course my happy youth, my good health, and my power of work. Out of the depths of my feeling of happiness there grew up gradually within me an understanding of the saying of Jesus that we must not treat our lives as being for ourselves alone. Whoever is spared personal pain must feel himself called to help in diminishing the pain of others. We must all carry our share of the misery which lies upon the world. Darkly and confusedly this thought worked in me, and sometimes it left me, so that I breathed freely and fancied once more that I was to become completely the lord of my own life. But the little cloud had risen above the horizon . . . and at last it hid the whole sky."[1]

When he was 21, one morning at Günsbach, his home in Alsace, during the Whitsun holidays, he suddenly came to the decision

"that I should consider myself justified in living till I was thirty for science and art, in order to devote myself from that time forward to the direct service of humanity. Many a time already had I tried to determine what meaning lay hidden for me in the saying of Jesus, 'Whosoever would save his life shall lose it, and whosoever shall lose his life for my sake and the Gospel's shall save it'. Now the

[1] *Memoirs of Childhood and Youth*, pp. 81-82.

answer was found. In addition to the outward, I now had inward happiness."[1]

He was widely known in many countries of Europe for his books and their translations; he was an appreciated preacher at one of the churches of Strasbourg; he occupied two Professors' chairs at the University; he was Principal of the residential college for students of theology; he was organist of the Strasbourg, Paris and Barcelona Bach Societies; he was the famous biographer of Bach; a writer and supreme authority on organ-building; a lecturer welcomed at many universities. He it was, for instance, who delivered the Funeral Oration on Nietzsche before the Sorbonne in Paris. He might easily have argued that he was doing so much useful work that his boyish resolve might be forgotten. But it was as vigorous as ever, and meanwhile his course had become clear. The Professor became once more a student, devoting himself to the study of medicine and surgery until, early in 1913, at the age of 38, he took a degree for the fourth time and immediately set out for Lambaréné in French Equatorial Africa with all his brilliant career apparently abandoned just as he was in his prime.

Now it was not for himself that Schweitzer was losing his life, but for humanity, for the ideals and the salvation of unborn generations. Many great thinkers have believed it is their part to think, to write their thoughts, to inspire others to action. By ordinary standards that is enough—a very great achievement. But for Albert Schweitzer it was not enough. He himself must translate his thought into action, he himself was in honour bound

[1] *My Life and Thought*, p. 103.

The Path to Reconstruction

to pay for all that was good and beautiful in his life by doing all he could to bear his share of the burden of the world's woe. And he must do this by going to where there was the most helpless of all misery, without questioning the value of the primitive lives whose suffering he would alleviate. In a world where nearly all of us are trying to get and to take all we can, his constant, unfailing aim has been to give, and to give where there is the greatest need. He keeps nothing back for himself, not even his privacy. He gives everything and gives all the time, and as Dr. Kraus, Professor of Philosophy at the University of Prague, says in his book on Schweitzer:[1] "Solche Denker, die ihr ethisches Denken in Tat umsetzen, sind die mächtigsten Faktoren der Weltgeschichte. . . ." ("Thinkers of this kind, who translate their ethical thought into action, are the most powerful factors in world history. . . .") Further he writes:

"Wherein lies the significance of Albert Schweitzer? Without doubt all that he has achieved for Art, Science and Religion is interesting and valuable. But more enduring and more valuable than all this is what he is accomplishing by the force of his personality and his ethical will. Humanity is rich in men who render great services in the individual fields and specialized departments of human knowledge and achievement. But it has been and is poor in great selfless characters who carry a light to follow, poor too in men of strong ethical will-power. Such a man is Albert Schweitzer. Dyrssen aptly writes: 'This is the deepest significance of what Albert Schweitzer did when

[1] Oskar Kraus, *Albert Schweitzer, sein Werk und seine Weltanschauung* (Prag, 1929), p. 13.

he turned his back on Europe after showing it the tragedy of its civilization. Knowledge is nothing; but only in sacrifice can action become fruitful and lead to the change which brings forth a new and better reality.' Knowledge is nothing; that is to say knowledge alone, bare intellectualism without ethical will. Ethical will, on the other hand, is the most beneficent force in world history. We are taught this by the life and sufferings of Jesus, of which the after-effects last for thousands of years. In the activities of Schweitzer for instance the moral energy of Christ lives on. This is the pattern to which Schweitzer directs us, reminding us that we need not be in agreement about our world-view and our religion, but that we must agree in reverence for all religions and the spiritual element in the world, and in reverence for the mysteries of creation around us, and that we must agree too about our outlook on life and ethics, in our enthusiasm for civilization and humanity. He teaches us that the ethic of selfless devotion is independent of creed. He restores to us faith in humanity and the unity of our civilization in the era of world-war, of murder by poison-gas, of national and racial hatred, of imperialism and capitalism and the dictatorship of class-hatred and their war of annihilation waged against all that is of the spirit."[1]

Schweitzer has never had any private or inherited income, yet his enterprise has always been absolutely independent. He started out with a sum equal to about £600 saved by frugal living, a calculation that this would last for two years—and faith in the future. He has always had to earn and collect for himself, largely by laborious letter-writing, the means to run the hospital with its ever-

[1] *Ibid.*, p. 73.

increasing number of patients. There is no religious or other society behind him and he gets no government grant.

And he did not go forth in any smug spirit, preening himself with the consciousness that he was sacrificing his career and happiness to do good to "those poor black people". He went saying,

"We are not free to confer benefits on these people, or not, as we please; it is our duty. Anything we give them is not benevolence, but atonement. . . . When we have done all that is in our power, we shall not have atoned for the thousandth part of our guilt. . . ."[1]

As in the Middle Ages cathedral windows taught the illiterate masses the Bible stories they could not read for themselves, so does the hospital set amid the swamps and jungle of the Dark Continent teach the philosophy of reverence for life to those who fail to read the printed word.

That Dr. Schweitzer, then a subject of Germany, which still held Alsace, chose a French colony for his activity is simply explained by the fact that there the need appeared greatest, for he is convinced that neither questions of nationality nor questions of religious creed, nor any other questions which needlessly divide man from man, should be mixed up with, or interfere with, the simple duties of man to man. He does not belong to any one nation or to any one sect; he belongs to humanity. It must be noted that this too is another cardinal tenet and practical aspect of his whole philosophy. This absolute universality, this

[1] *On the Edge of the Primeval Forest*, 7th impression, p. 172.

constant striving to break down all differences, all barriers, all obstacles which divide and embitter men of different races, different allegiances and different faiths should make his thought extraordinarily valuable to all whose minds are, or will be, occupied with the reconstruction of the post-war world. For truly in this age of disconsolate wandering in search of a creed to live by there is no man whose life and works better repay study. There gleams through his acts, as through his pages, a golden thread of hope for the unity and brotherhood of all who share in the glorious phenomenon called Life.

What a spiritual leader for the nations of the whole world is here in this great and completely free man, who is not disqualified from any activity in any place by allegiance to any one nation or to any one body of men, and not even debarred from any one form of beneficent activity by his own mastery in another.

CHAPTER II

The Decline of Civilization

WHEN he was a mere boy studying at the University of Strasbourg, Albert Schweitzer had already begun to feel misgivings about the theory current in those days that human progress is automatically and constantly going on without our needing to trouble about it. He was surprised and shocked to find that inhumane ideas and inhumane actions, whether on the part of individuals or of governments, failed to arouse popular indignation, while there were many other signs of intellectual and spiritual fatigue and also a recrudescence of superstition. He felt that we were largely living on the achievements of past generations, and were even allowing our inherited spiritual wealth to melt away in our hands, with the result that in our cultural life we had already sunk to a lower level of civilization than that which had been previously reached.

It was in 1899, when he was in his 25th year, that he first determined to write a book on the subject, but it was not until fifteen years later, after the 1914 war had begun, that he found time in the long quiet evenings near the Equator to apply himself to this work, the scope of

which had of course greatly widened under the influence
of events. Hence its title instead of being only *Wir Epigonen*
("We Inheritors of the Past"), as was originally intended,
became *Der Verfall und Wiederaufbau der Kultur* ("The
Decay and the Restoration of Civilization") for the first
volume, and *Kultur und Ethik* ("Civilization and Ethics")
for the second of a *Philosophy of Civilization* planned for
four in all. The third volume *The World-view of Reverence
for Life*, and the fourth, which is to treat of the Civilized
State, still remain unpublished, though in large part
written. The tragic trend of events in the last twenty years
has made the author, I think, feel that it is impossible as
yet to express his thought in such a way that men will
listen to what is so diametrically opposed to current
thought and opinion. But, now again in Africa, he is still
working on these books, and it may be hoped that now
men's minds, schooled in suffering, are more recipient of
thoughts that matter and are turning to "reconstruction",
he will soon deem it advisable to allow publication.

The two first volumes appeared in 1923 in Germany
and in England. The warning they contain was there for
all to read. They were well reviewed, went into several
editions on the Continent and two editions in England.[1]
The same warning was often repeated, especially and very
notably in the Goethe Memorial Oration at Frankfurt
on March 22nd, 1932, the occasion I believe of his last
visit to Germany, and again in the Gifford Lectures at
Edinburgh in 1934 and 1935. But it passed unheeded.
People were perhaps too much occupied with thoughts

[1] I believe, but at the present time have no means of verifying the
belief, that Kagawa translated the volumes into Japanese.

of the Doctor of the African jungle, or with the Doctor of Music, the great organist and famous biographer of J. S. Bach, or with the eminent Doctor of Divinity who had startled the theologians of all Europe with his incontrovertible new theories about the life of Jesus and the work of St. Paul, to concern themselves with the ethics of the equally famous Doctor of Philosophy, the prophet and seer of his age, the apostle of a nobler civilization. Yet posterity will probably regard *Civilization and Ethics* as, so far, his greatest single achievement.

No reader of the slender first volume can fail to be impressed with the masterly analysis of the causes of the catastrophe we are experiencing and with the prophetic insight of its forebodings, forebodings which are expressed with increased intensity of gloom in the Memorial Oration on Goethe, begun at the exact hour of Goethe's death one hundred years before. How awe-inspiring was the occasion of its delivery! The great opera-house in the poet's birthplace was packed to its utmost capacity with listeners so spellbound by the gravity of the only speaker that for sixty-five minutes one could, as the phrase goes, have heard a pin drop but for the sound of his voice. Again and again he referred to the present time as "grausig" (gruesome, frightful), and he proclaimed that a gigantic repetition of the Faust-drama was being played on the world-stage.

"In tausend Flammen brennt die Hütte von Philemon und Baucis! In tausendfacher Gewalttätigkeit und tausendfachem Morden treibt entmenschte Gesinnung ihr frevelhaftes Spiel! In tausend Fratzen grinst uns Mephistopheles an! In tausendfacher Weise hat sich die Menschheit dazu bringen lassen, das natürliche Verhältnis zur Wirklichkeit aufzugeben und ihr Heil in den Zauberformeln irgendeiner Wirtschafts- und Sozialmagie zu suchen, die die Möglichkeit aus dem wirtschaftlichen und sozialen Elend herauszukommen nur immer in weitere Ferne rückt!

"Und der grausige Sinn dieser Zauberformeln, welcher Art von Wirtschafts- und Sozialmagie sie auch angehören, ist immer eben dieser, dass der einzelne sein materielles und geistiges Eigendasein aufzugeben und nur noch als ein Angehöriger einer materiell und geistig restlos über ihn verfügenden Vielheit zu existieren habe."

("In thousands of flames the cottage of Philemon and Baucis is burning! In thousandfold acts of violence and thousandfold deeds of murder a mentality which has lost all human qualities wages its wanton sport! With a thousand grimaces Mephistopheles grins in our faces! In thousandfold ways man has let himself be led to renounce his natural relationship to reality and to seek his weal in the magic formulas of some economic or social system which only thrusts still further the possibility of escape from economic and social misery.

"And the terrible significance of these magic formulae, to whatever school of economic and social theory they may belong, is always that the individual has to surrender his material and spiritual personal existence, and may continue to live only as belonging body and soul to a plurality which controls him absolutely.")

The impending catastrophe which he then lamented is now an accomplished, unquestioned fact. Must the warning again pass unheeded? Lord Halifax said a few months ago in America that the present war is a "mortal clash of two philosophies". We all know a great deal now about one of those philosophies, the herd philosophy of massed

2

force. But are we quite clear, are we at all definite, about the other? Are we clear about what the contrary philosophy really is, or about what in practice it might be? Let us take Dr. Schweitzer as our guide to some clearer thinking about it.

According to his view, we are now living in a period when civilization is in actual process of decay. This process was not brought about by the war of 1914–18. The war, ultimately resulting from commercial rivalry, from scientific developments and machinery, and itself rendered devastating by scientific invention, was one of the symptoms, not one of the causes, of this process of decay. Since then we have been carried and are still being carried downstream as in the swirling waters below a cataract.

Ultimately, this has all come about from a want of reflection upon what civilization actually is. All the many books written about it have been concerned only with its historical origins and development, and such works have served only to confirm and strengthen our arrogant belief in the value of our forms of what we call civilization, and have blinded us to its defects. Those who had misgivings have been forced to keep silence. "The great works on philosophy and ehtics in recent years have all tried to avoid absolute ethics by concentrating on a type which should apply only socially."[1]

Earlier, in the eighteenth century, ethical, rational ideas had been at work, and the steady progress which had been made in the direction of a true, well-based civilization seemed to justify a hope that such a civilization would

[1] "The Ethics of Reverence for Life", Albert Schweitzer in *Christendom*, Winter 1936. (Quarterly, Chicago.)

eventually be realized. The Rationalists in England and the men of the "Aufklärung" in Germany were certain of the existence and activity of a benign Divine Purpose, and from this they inferred an ethic which they regarded as the divine law for man. They hoped through ethical activity finally to realize the Kingdom of God on earth.

But from the middle of the nineteenth century the impetus in this direction gradually died down as if it were exhausted. In the period which then began, says Schweitzer, the determining factor in the movement of thought was the abandonment by philosophy of the leadership of popular opinion which it had exerted for over a century. It failed to produce the ethical and religious ideas of which men feel the need for their enlightenment and guidance, and it failed to meet the criticisms of logical thinking while still clinging to an optimistic ethical outlook on life expressed with a naïve dogmatism which roused increasing incredulity and finally made people declare that thought had gone bankrupt.

Kant (1724-1804), Fichte (1762-1814), Hegel (1770-1831) and others had tried to stem the tide and to give new reasons for faith in the ethical ideals of Rationalism. But meanwhile the Natural Sciences had been advancing and gaining strength, and men exalted scientific truth and reality to refute all ideals that were based only on imagination. A distinction thus came more or less consciously to be drawn between scientific truth on the one hand and ethical and religious convictions founded in feeling and belief on the other. These latter came to be regarded as second-class truths with only a relative value. Personal morality was looked upon as outside the sphere of reason.

The age of philosophic dogmatism was at an end. Rationalism was dead, and along with it the optimistic and ethical convictions which it had originated concerning the purpose of the universe and of human life. Nevertheless these old beliefs did continue to exert some posthumous influence, with the result that men had no inkling of the disaster that was inevitably impending.

Finally, about the middle of the nineteenth century, philosophy, which had been like a workman engaged in actually building the fabric of civilization, became very largely a science concerned merely with sifting the conclusions of the natural and historical sciences, as if accumulating them as material for some future theory of the universe which it never produced. Thus it lost the power of spontaneous and reasoned elemental thought and almost degenerated into being a mere history of past thought—the history of philosophy instead of philosophy itself—for it abandoned its proper function of finding a true and serviceable outlook upon life. Having nothing constructive to say to mankind, it did, however, continue to play a certain academical part in schools and universities. But even in exercising this function it looked down upon the philosophy of the past for its naïveté and upon anything in the nature of popular philosophy for its simplicity. It ignored the fact that the value of any philosophy is to be measured by its capacity to transform itself into a living way of thought to guide the lives of the masses. For all truth that is profound is simple and can be reproduced in simple terms.

What is there left of the achievements of our recent philosophy when it is stripped of the tinsel of learning?

Schweitzer replies that it has attempted to philosophize about everything except civilization, and that in so doing it has failed even to notice that it, and the age along with it, was slipping further and further from civilization. In the hour of danger, philosophy, the watchman who should have warned us, has been asleep. So nothing has been done to defend our heritage, to defend the ideas of true civilization which have been handed down to us from the past.

The fatal thing about what we now call our civilization is that it has developed far more materially than spiritually; whereas what is essential in civilization is not to be found in material achievements. What is essential is that individuals should always keep in mind the ideals of the perfecting of man and the improvement of the social and political conditions of all peoples, and that they should believe in and aim at the spiritual and ethical progress of humanity. Whether there is more or less material achievement is not essential to civilization. The important thing is that thought should keep control over facts.

But although the failure of thinking has been the decisive factor in the decay of civilization, it has not been alone responsible. The capacity for sound development in civilization by the modern man has been reduced by the injurious nature of the circumstances in which he is placed. Material and spiritual freedom are closely connected, and civilization postulates free men, for by free men alone can it be conceived and realized. But in modern man material freedom and with it the capacity for thinking are alike diminished. Material achievements have made man freer than before in his relation to natural forces, but at the same time have reduced the independence of individual existences. For example: machinery has transformed artisans into factory hands. More and more human beings have been gathered into great masses separated from their mother earth and from nature, and have consequently suffered damage in their spiritual nature. And to lack of liberty has been added the further handicap of overstrain, so that for some generations past many individuals have lived only as unceasing workers, not as free human beings.

The consequence of overwork and over-industrialization in all grades of society is manifested in the stunting of the spiritual faculties. This process begins even in childhood, because the parents, inextricably absorbed in toil, have no time and no energy to devote themselves in a normal way to their children. Similarly, when the child becomes a worker himself, the strain on him is so great that he cannot concentrate on anything serious in his hours of leisure; hence it becomes a physical necessity to seek only complete idleness or only those forms of entertainment which demand no exercise of judgment or thought and merely enable him to forget himself. Again, the places of amusement and the press have in turn increasingly pandered to this lowered intellectual standard, and we have only to compare the daily papers of the present[1] with those of fifty years ago to recognize the deterioration. In social life conversation is usually limited to generalities, and as a rule nothing original is given out or expected. Schweitzer's comment on this is:

"How much I suffer from the way we spend so much of our time uselessly instead of talking seriously about

[1] Dr. Schweitzer was writing in, or before, 1923.

serious things, and getting to know each other well as striving and suffering, hoping and believing mortals! I often feel it to be absolutely wrong to sit like that, as it were with a mask on. Many a time I ask myself how far we can carry this well-bred behaviour without harm to our sincerity."[1]

This prevailing superficiality, due partly to the decline of philosophical thought and partly to the decline of economic freedom, has resulted in a generally lowered conception of what man might be, and we now see to what a pass it has led us.

Yet another hindrance to civilization in modern man is his one-sidedness and therefore his incompleteness as an individual. The enormous increase in knowledge has involved specialization, so that not the whole man, but only one aspect of his capacity is brought into play; hence his other creative capacities and his artistic instincts perish for want of use. Nowhere is the defect consequent on excessive specialization so evident as in science, and this in turn has unfortunate repercussions on education, because teachers fail to make their pupils understand the proper correlation of one individual branch of knowledge with another. And in every direction excessive organization, with its rules and regulations, necessarily restricts the scope of individual initiative. The elementary school teacher, to take one example, is in many countries far less free than he used to be, and hence his teaching is often lifeless and impersonal.

But worse still, man is in danger of losing his humanity and his power of personal response to his fellows. As a

[1] *Memoirs of Childhood and Youth*, p. 76.

23

result of hurry and overcrowding and overstrain, he meets them as strangers, and no longer realizes how unnatural and how outrageous this artificiality is. When we cease to be conscious that every human being concerns us just because he is our fellow-human, then the foundations of civilization and ethics are beginning to be undermined. For the past two generations there has developed a social mentality which estranges individuals from natural human feeling. Standoffishness and lack of interest and sympathy are regarded, not as rudeness, nor even as unnatural, but as correct behaviour. The human worth and human dignity of all men, from being overlooked, ceases to be recognized and so gets actually denied to vast groups who are regarded not as men, but only as raw material for certain ends. The light-hearted way, for instance, in which people had gradually come to talk of war and conquest showed that they had no more regard for the fate of individuals than they would have if war were only a game of chess. Similarly, in regard to the coloured races, in recent decades men have sometimes written and publicly spoken in terms which suggested they were hardly human at all. Again, in modern education, the duty of humanity, the most elementary thing in the training of personality, now receives but scant attention. It was not always thus. Robinson Crusoe, for example, a favourite hero of past generations of young people all over Europe, is constantly concerned with the question of humane conduct. When in self-defence he is forced to kill, he tries to sacrifice as few of his enemies' lives as possible.

Yet another hindrance to civilization is the over-organization of public life. Personalities and ideas are subordinated to institutions, whereas it should be the other way about. Our spiritual and mental life now runs its course within organizations, and from childhood up, man learns to think with his group. In the eighteenth century ideas had to be justified by the individual reason; but now consideration is given only to the views which prevail in organized social groups. The individual thus tends to take it for granted that the outlook of his nation, his creed, his political party, his group, is beyond criticism, and he thus becomes so lost in the mentality of the mass that he almost ceases to lead an independent mental existence. And yet he is quite unconscious that this abnormal susceptibility to group influence is a weakness, for he thinks that by action in combination with others he is helping to guard the greatness of modern man. It is largely because the majority have in this way renounced the right of thinking for themselves, and are guided only by the opinion of their groups, that freedom of thought has to so great an extent gone out of use.

The ethics which should control the individual cannot be translated into an ethic of society. The first is absolute, the second relative. The valuation of humane conduct is different in the two systems, for humanity consists in never sacrificing a person to a purpose, and the community cannot always consider, and ought not always to consider, the individual. Even a society with a relatively high standard of ethics is a danger to the morality of its members; and if it exercises an excessively strong influence on individuals, their personal conceptions of moral conduct may be ruined. That is what happens in the social systems of the present generation, whose ethical conscience is first blunted by biological and sociological considerations and then is fatally corrupted by nationalism. Thus the greatest error of all ethical thought hitherto has been the failure to recognize the essential difference between the ethics required for the individual and the ethics established by society. The result has been that personal ethics are sacrificed. This must come to an end. It must be recognized that the two standpoints are at variance.

A basic principle of morality must therefore be established in order that personal morality can logically and successfully try conclusions with the morality of the community, for we shall regain the freedom of the spirit only when individuals have once more asserted their independence and discovered a more natural and dignified relationship to one another and to the organizations which have entangled their souls. But meanwhile there has been so little realization of the spiritual misery in which we are sunk, that the process of spreading opinions which have no foundation in thought is constantly intensified and applauded.

In so far as independent thought was abandoned, faith in truth was inevitably lost; for when man surrenders his personal opinion, he surrenders also his personal moral judgment. He suppresses any misgivings he may feel in order that he may agree with the mass of his fellows as to what is good and what is bad. He acquires a power of making excuses for all that is stupid, cruel and unjust in the conduct of his own group or nation. Public opinion helps him in this by disseminating the theory that the actions of the community are to be measured rather by the standards of expediency than by those of morality. The demoralization of the individual by the mass is thus in full swing.

And for all these tendencies which Dr. Schweitzer enumerates, he says philosophy has shown no understanding, and has offered no guidance or help to their victims. The hideous truth that with the progress of history and economic development, civilization becomes not easier but more difficult has been left unrealized and therefore unspoken.

What then *is* civilization? The question seems never to have been answered, because, it seems, it was never really put. Because we were supposed to possess civilization, it has been thought unnecessary to define it. Speaking quite generally, Schweitzer says it may be defined as the material and spiritual progress both of individuals and of communities in such a way that for both the struggle for existence becomes less strenuous.

The struggle for existence has two aspects. Man has to maintain his position not only in and against nature, but among and against his fellows. The struggle on both planes will grow less intense as reason gains the supremacy (1) over external nature and (2) over human nature. This second form of progress, however, though less apparent, is the more vital, because only the mastery of reason over human thought can guarantee that men shall not employ against each other the forces of nature which have come under their control. Only when he consciously distinguishes between what is essential and what is non-essential in civilization is man normally conscious of possessing it. And in what does the supremacy of reason in human thought consist? It means that individuals and communities shall allow their will to be determined by the material and spiritual welfare of the whole of mankind, and that is equivalent to saying that their aims are moral, or determined by sound ethical principles. Thus what is vital and what is essential is not material, but moral or ethical, progress.

For many decades until the middle of the nineteenth century, the material and moral or ethical forces of progress were at work side by side, but moral and ethical energy then died away, whilst the conquests of the mind in the material sphere were marvellously rapid. For some time these were enjoyed without any perception of the results accruing from the cessation of ethical development —and were enjoyed without any suspicion of the storms that in consequence were brewing within and between the nations. In this way our own age had come to believe that civilization consists first and foremost in scientific, technical and artistic achievement, and that it can get along without ethics or with a minimum of morality. It has reacted to facts without any appeal to reason and so has laid no foundation and made no plans for its future.

Our blindness is further intensified by our misplaced belief in our historical sense. The historical sense, rightly understood, implies critical objectivity in relation to distant and near events alike, and this is a capacity which even our historians tend not to exercise. When the past is near enough to have any connection with the present, their estimate of it is inclined to be affected by their national, religious, social and economic standpoint. Instead of being educative forces, our historians act simply

as men of learning. The past is even misused to the extent
of legitimizing in it our claims, opinions, feelings and
passions, to the extent of even fabricating history for
popular use in order to support national and religious
ideas. Many school history books are actual nurseries of
historical mendacity. But if the supremacy of reason is
abandoned, this misuse of history becomes of course a
necessity, for if the ideas and opinions which govern us
cannot be based on reason, there is no alternative left but
to provide them with "historical" foundations instead.

In this way, from our false conception of reality and our
false historical sense was born the nationalism to which we
must attribute the external catastrophe which now com-
pletes the decline of our civilization. Nationalism, says Dr.
Schweitzer, is an ignoble form of patriotism exalted to
such a pitch of imbecility that it bears to patriotism that
is noble and healthy the same relationship as do the
delusions of a madman to the normal convictions of a
sane person.

It was at the beginning of the nineteenth century that
philosophy established the right of the nation-state,
believing that as a natural and homogeneous organism it
was the form of organization best qualified to make a
reality of the ideal of the civilized state. Fichte, in his
Addresses to the German Nation (1808), emphasizes that the
highest task before the nation is to foster the continuous
development of the purely human element in its life. It
must seek its greatness as the representative of the ideas
which are able to bring healing to the peoples of the
world. Its citizens are urged to belong to it, not with the
lower, narrow form of national patriotism, but with the

higher patriotism, that patriotism which does not value external greatness and power, but makes its aim "the blossoming of the Eternal and the Divine" on earth. The feeling for nationality is thus to be under the guardianship of reason, morality and civilization, and the cult of narrow patriotism as such is to be regarded as barbaric.

When civilization was on the decline, the idea of nationalism survived the decay of all other ideals because it had been translated into something tangible and "actual". Thus it came about that our age now concentrates all its enthusiasm upon this one idea of nationalism, now independent of and in revolt from the tutelage of all moral considerations. Nationalism claims that it follows a policy of "Realpolitik"—a policy of tangible practical results. But in reality it is a policy, supported by popular passion, a dogmatic policy of idealized overvaluation of various economic considerations and various territorial ambitions. For example, in order to be able to dispute the possession of a few tens of millions or less, a state will spend thousands of millions on armaments and on war.

And finally, nationalism, not content with abandoning all attempts to establish a really civilized humanity as advocated by Fichte, proceeded to distort the very conception of civilization itself by proclaiming national civilization! In old days civilization simply was civilization, and every civilized people strove to possess it, so far as it could, in its purest and most highly developed form. The claim to national civilization is an artificial and unhealthy misgrowth, only possible because civilized peoples have lost their simple, healthy nature, and are guided by artificial theories instead of by natural instincts. There is now so much dogmatizing and hair-splitting about racial differences that people become obsessed as by an imaginary disease. Anything valuable in a personality or in an achievement is attributed to the peculiar excellence of the national character, and there is no length of absurdity to which men are not led by this arrogant national vanity. And further, national civilization is not content to be limited to its own nation, but feels it to be its mission to force its so-called blessings on to other peoples. Nations seek markets for their culture just as they do for their manufactures, and in the competition between rival national civilizations it goes ill with civilization itself. The peoples that inherited the civilization of the Greco-Roman world were once inseparably one in culture, and their spiritual affinity is still evident in their common spiritual decadence. The ever-increasing differences between them in this latest age are apparent because of the fall in the whole level of civilized thought. "When the tide ebbs, shallows which separate bodies of deep water become visible; while the tide is flowing they are out of sight."

A further spiritual defect, blinding us to what is happening, is that we have a misplaced confidence in facts, optimistically thinking they are sure to arrange themselves in the interests of progress. This false optimism is largely to be attributed to the teaching of Hegel, the spiritual father of our sense of realism. But Hegel lived in the time of Rationalism and believed not only in the power of ethical reason, but in a spiritual progress which nothing could stop. The facts in themselves, however, are constantly contradicting this theory of spontaneous progress.

Along with our reliance on facts goes our reliance on institutions, as though, if only our institutions could be perfected, progress would take care of itself! People of all shades of political opinion believe that from new institutions a new spirit will arise.

Lastly, for many even of the most serious minds the true relation between the spiritual and the actual has been reversed, so that they believe that facts can give birth to things of spiritual value, whereas all experience goes to show that it is the spirit which gives birth to everything, and that institutions, unless informed by the spirit, are in themselves of little import.

The only conceivable way therefore of reconstructing our world is that under the old conditions we should become new men with a new spirit, and then, with a new attitude of thought, that we should so smooth out the differences in and between the nations as to render really civilized conditions once more possible. Meanwhile, just as we feel that the impulse to action is a necessary element of our existence, so we have to strive to attain to an outlook on life in which this impulse will find its justification and be able to realize ideals inspired by the spirit of true humanity. For this purpose we can find firm ground under our feet only in the ideals of ethical reason. What is going on to-day in and between the nations throws glaring light on this truth. Never in all history was there a period so mad, and the explanation quite simply is the fact that we tried to get along with a civilization that is destitute of sound moral values and sound ethical principles, or of any moral philosophy based on reason.

Is there then any path at all that can lead us from bar-

barism back to civilization? The non-moral conception of civilization regards all symptoms of decay as the normal symptoms of old age, and believes there is nothing to be done to arrest it. According to such a theory, it is not civilization itself, but only *a* civilization that is dissolving, and so some new form of civilization is expected to arise in some new race. But the world no longer has new peoples in reserve as it formerly had. All peoples now have some share in our existing forms of civilization, and all suffer from the same disease as we do. So it is really the civilization of all mankind that is in danger.

But it need not be lost. As soon as ethical energy can once more get to work in our thought, decline will cease, and regeneration will begin. The difficulties are indeed so enormous that only a very strong faith in the power of the ethical spirit can give us any hope. For, to begin with, the unthinking optimism of the masses has to be over-come, along with the equally unthinking pessimism which refuses to believe in the possibility of spiritual progress.

Then again, reconstruction is more difficult than building something new. The ideals men need are not new; they are old ideals which have come to be regarded as having been "used up". History suggests that our task is impossible. "Never yet", it says, "have worn-out ideas risen to new power among the peoples who had used them up." But the fact that this has never happened with ideals that really are worn out does not prove that the reconstruction of old ideals can never be achieved in the future. We must study history from a new angle, and by the laws of spiritual life find out why the essential thought of civilization has lost its power of bringing conviction, and why traditional truths have become mere phrases. The recognition that civilization must still be founded on world-view, and that it can spring only from a spiritual awakening and the ethical will of the masses, may make us realize the difficulties in the way of attaining it; but at the same time this recognition clears the undertaking from all considerations of possibility or impossibility.

The great task therefore of the human spirit is to create a world-view, for it is in its world-view that the ideas, thoughts and deeds of an age ultimately have their roots.

To-day the great majority of people not only fail to attain to any thought-out world-view or philosophy, but are not even conscious that they derive their ideas and opinions from such a source. All thinking ultimately rests on the world-view of the thinker, and every age, consciously or unconsciously, lives on the thoughts of its thinkers. Plato was wrong in saying the philosophers of a state should be its rulers. Thinkers are the officers of the general staff who sit in the background and work out the problems of the struggle. The men who play a part in public life are their subordinate officers, who convert their general directions into orders of the day. If the thinkers of any age produce a world-view which has value, ideas which bring about progress then become disseminated, whereas, if the thinkers fail, decadence in one form or another will set in. The fall of the Roman Empire was really due to the want of a philosophy of life which could preserve it. Stoicism, grand as it was, is based on resignation, and so could not secure progress.

In the eighteenth century, during the reigns of insignificant princes with insignificant statesmen, a movement of progress unique in the history of the world did begin among the peoples of Europe, because the thinkers of the time created an outlook on life which spread valuable ideas among their fellows. But now we are squandering the heritage of the past and living among ruins because we cannot complete the building our forefathers began.

Reconstruction, therefore, can begin only with reconstruction of our world-view or outlook on life. So with what conditions must a world-view comply in order to create civilization anew? First, it must result from thought and reason, for it is only when it has been turned over in the thought of the many and recognized as truth that it can attain to the force of communicable and lasting conviction. In much with which it reproached Rationalism the reaction of the early nineteenth century was justified. Nevertheless, by its ridicule of details it demolished a whole structure which in spite of its imperfections was one of the greatest manifestations of the spiritual life of mankind. Under the influence of Rationalism, through all ranks of society there had been faith in thought and there had been reverence for truth. Reason is not dry intellectualism, but the synthesis or sum-total of all our spiritual and mental functions in living interaction. The outlook on life which reason produces comprehends all that we think and feel about the destiny of humanity, and gives direction and value to our existence. If therefore we venture once more to seek the light of reason, we shall no longer remain incapable of enthusiasm, but shall experience the deep and noble passion that is inspired by great ideals. All real progress in the world has been due to reason, and all movements that have supplanted Rationalism have been far inferior to it in their achievements; for incomplete and unsatisfactory as were its results, the principle which it established that world-view must be based on thought, and on thought alone, is the only true principle. Philosophical, historical and scientific questions to which it was not yet equal overwhelmed Rationalism like an avalanche. Now a new world-view, a new outlook on life, founded on reason, must work its way out of the chaos which surrounds us.

But is there any hope whatever that this is possible in a world where so large a mass of mankind neither thinks nor gives any encouragement to thinkers? Doubt whether the great majority of people can ever be led to reflection is justified indeed, if we consider man of the present day. But he, with his diminished need and diminished capacity for thought, is only a temporary pathological phenomenon, and we may still believe that most human beings are really endowed with the power to think, for this is usually evident in the young when they begin to lead independent personal lives. Of course there will always be leaders and led in the matter of world-view as in any other; but the decisive question will be, whether the influence of the leaders results in the dependence or in the independence of the led.

If there are to be large numbers of people with independent minds, it is obvious that the preservation and stimulation of individuality are all-important. "Schweitzer", says Barthel,[1] "has great reverence for in-

[1] Ernst Barthel, *Elsässische Geistesschicksale* (Heidelberg, 1928), p. 231.

dividuality and values all its rights as inviolable and sacred. In this respect one may say he is a democrat. But on the other hand he feels himself completely alien to 'democracy' in its form of a political movement originating in the French Revolution, because of its disregard for the rights of the individual. The terribly impersonal element in political democracy is essentially foreign to his standpoint, and this is the very reason why he prizes the rights of the individual so highly. His sentiments are 'individual' in a profound and spiritual sense, and therefore almost anti-democratic; for it is precisely the 'Demos' which aims at the destruction of individuality."

CHAPTER III

Reconstruction

RECONSTRUCTION then must begin with the attainment of a world-view founded on reflection and reason. Next, this world-view must be optimistic and ethical, if the ideas and convictions of true civilization are to find in it a foundation based on a sound system of ethics. An optimistic world-view is an outlook on life which affirms that the world and life have value in themselves; and from this belief will come the impulse to raise life, in so far as we can influence it, to its highest value. Every kind of social and scientific activity will be involved. When the outlook on life is pessimistic, ethics are concerned only with the self-fulfilment of the individual, but under the influence of an optimistic, life-affirming outlook the aim of ethics expands beyond the self-perfecting of the individual, because there is confidence that the world-process has somehow or other a spiritual and purposeful aim, and that the improvement of the general relations of the world and of society promotes the spiritual and moral perfecting of the individual. It is the interaction of ethics with an optimistic outlook on life that produces civilization, and the future of civilization depends on whether it is possible for thought to reach a world-view based on these foundations. Again and again philosophers imagined that they had succeeded in solving this problem; but again and again their illusion was shattered. Nevertheless, their aim was lofty, and their work has given us insight into the causes of their failure.

Why then *did* they fail? They failed because, diverging from their true course, they sought to interpret man's life in terms of the universe instead of in terms of life. In Schweitzer's own words,[1] "Working purposefully ourselves toward certain ends, we assume that the Creative Force in the world is doing likewise. Yet, when we try to define its goal, we cannot do so . . . there is no co-ordinated definite end to be observed, even though we think that there should be. We like to imagine that man is nature's goal, but facts do not support that belief." After the discoveries of Copernicus, Kepler and Galileo, the earth could no longer be regarded as the centre and main concern of the universe. The beginning of all spiritual life is a fearless faith in truth, however disturbing it may be, and an open confession of that faith, and truth compels us to face this fact that the material universe has no optimistic and no ethical meaning for us. We can see no aim or purpose in what happens within it—nothing corresponding to the ethical feeling in our hearts. On a small planet among millions of stars there is life. "But the Creative Force does not concern itself about preserving life."[2] A change of temperature, a rise in the level of the ocean, an alteration in the composition of the atmo-

[1] "The Ethics of Reverence for Life", by Albert Schweitzer, in *Christendom*, vol. i, No. 2 (Chicago, 1936).   [2] *Ibid.*

sphere—and all would be over. We have no notion of what is the significance of man's existence on the earth, that earth which is a mere speck of dust in the infinite cosmos. How then can we presume to attempt to explain the universe?

Again, nature is a force which seems at the same time marvellously creative and senselessly destructive. "So that for us there can really be no question of activity in co-operation with the Spirit of the Universe; but only of devoting ourselves to an activity through which we may experience spiritual union with that Spirit."[1] Schweitzer would not, I am sure, ask us to renounce our dreams of "one far-off divine event to which the whole creation moves", for he tells us that although so far as knowledge goes he is a pessimist, in willing and hoping he is an optimist,[2] and he would probably say that what we know of the Creator within our own hearts justifies such a hope. But we dare not assert a hope of this kind as a fact.

Hitherto the word "Weltanschauung" has combined world-view and life-view, but we must give up this joint conception and recognize the two views as independent; for as a consequence of the combination we have become sceptical about our outlook on life, and the shock to the instinct for truth involved in an interpretation of the material universe has played a fatal part in the outlook on life of our time. We instinctively rebel against the dualism involved, a dualism to which all the problems of human thought ultimately go back, but we must accept the dualism of the facts, and, if we accept these facts as

[1] *Indian Thought and its Development*, p. 259.
[2] *My Life and Thought*, p. 279.

facts, we must confess that we are surrounded by enigmas. We can, however, also recognize that the facts can do us no harm and we can be satisfied to leave the enigmas unsolved.

Approaching the same difficulty from the standpoint of religion, Schweitzer says:

"All problems of religion ultimately go back to this one—the experience I have of God within myself differs from the knowledge concerning Him which I derive from the world. . . . The knowledge concerning God which is derived from Nature is always imperfect and inadequate, because we perceive the things in the world from without only. . . . In myself, on the other hand, I know things from within. . . . All the mysteries of the world and of my existence in the world may ultimately be left on one side unsolved and insoluble. . . . Let me express it in a simile. There is an ocean—cold water without motion. In this ocean, however, is the Gulf Stream, hot water, flowing from the Equator towards the Pole. Inquire of all scientists how it is physically imaginable that a stream of hot water flows between the waters of the ocean, which, so to speak, form its banks, the moving within the motionless, the hot within the cold: no scientist can explain it. Similarly there is the God of love within the God of the forces of the universe—one with Him, and yet so totally different. We let ourselves be seized and carried away by that vital stream."[1]

In the *Discourse on Goethe*, Schweitzer points out that Goethe, too, alone among the thinkers of his age, abandoned the hope of understanding the material universe,

[1] *Christianity and the Religions of the World*, p. 78.

and believed that only the Infinite revealed in nature and in his own heart has for man actuality and significance.

> "Was ist Unendlichkeit?
> Wie kannst du dich so quälen?
> Geh in dich selbst;
> Entbehrst du drin Unendlichkeit in Sein und Sinn
> So ist dir nicht zu helfen."

> ("What is Infinity?
> How canst thou so torture thyself?
> Look within!
> If there thou lack'st infinity in being and mind,
> No help for thee.")

What is the simple, immediate fact of which we are conscious? Surely not Descartes' "I think, therefore I exist", which says nothing about *what* I think, but "I am life which wills to live, in the midst of life which wills to live". This is the one essential thing we know about ourselves, and we take it as a matter of course, because an inner necessity has made it part of our mental make-up, so that we begin our lives in simple world- and life-affirmation. Our task is to try to get clear about what this means. In order to bring to their highest value our own lives and all kinds of life that we can influence, we must advance from the elementary fact of consciousness to a new and profounder form of life-affirmation. This will bid us not withdraw into ourselves, though by doing so we might enjoy rest; but to take a living, active interest in all that happens around us, though by doing this we shall be involved in a state of constant unrest.

When thought awakens, all kinds of problems arise, and we realize that disappointment and pain must be our lot, and that our activities generally seem to have as little result as if we had tried to plough the furrows of the sea. The resulting doubt and pessimism cause every thinking being at some time to question whether life is worth living, and to become familiar with the thought of suicide, though he does not allow others to suspect this, and rejects the thought from a feeling of instinctive repulsion, because the will-to-live is stronger than this pessimistic impulse. Even the logical pessimism of Brahmanism and Buddhism rejects it, the Buddha saying that it is not life, but only the *will* to live, to which we must put an end. Pessimism therefore is always inconsistent. Where, however, the profounder mentality of world- and life-affirmation is not definitely reached, the will-to-live is depreciated and loses force for the tasks of practical life. Enough energy may be left to go on living, but not enough to overcome pessimism, so that men subsist miserably on a little bit of happiness and many vain thoughts. Yet, even so, their will to live often asserts itself and becomes a kind of intoxication.

"Spring sunshine, trees in blossom, drifting clouds, fields of waving corn provoke it. A will-to-live which proclaims itself in many forms in magnificent phenomena all around them carries their own will-to-live along with it. Filled with delight, they want to take part in the mighty symphony they hear. They find the world beautiful. . . . But the transport passes. Hideous discords cause them once more to hear only noise where they thought they heard music. The beauty of nature is darkened for them by the suffering which they discover everywhere within it. Now they see once more that they are floating like shipwrecked mariners over a waste of waters. . . ."[1]

But the will-to-live is not limited for its support to knowledge of the external universe. It may find its means of subsistence within itself, and the ideas that are given with it should be accepted as a high and determining kind of knowledge. Its essential nature is a resolve to live to the full, and to realize the highest possible perfection.[2] In all nature, for example in a blade of grass or in a crystal, we see this impulse, this striving after perfection; "in everything that exists there is at work an imaginative force, which is determined by ideals". And we know that this is part of our own nature as well, and that we ought to obey it in conformity with the will-to-live that is in us. To be true to it, to allow it to develop to complete vitality, is what will decide the fate of our existence. Through world- and life-affirmation our will-to-live joins in pursuing the aims of the mysterious, universal will-to-live of which we ourselves are a manifestation, and thus we give our existence a meaning from within which is correlated with outward phenomena.

But all this does not lead to an easy-going, happy condition of confirmed optimism. The war between optimism and pessimism is never fought to a finish within us, but must go on all through our lives, and accordingly we have to be constantly on our guard against allowing any deterioration in our will-to-live.

[1] *Civilization and Ethics*, chap. xviii. (*N.B.*—The *first* English edition of this book contains many errors.)

[2] As Goethe puts it, "Zum höchsten Dasein immerfort zu streben" (*Faust*, Part II).

We have to realize that happiness does not depend on anything outside our own being, and our will-to-live must seek to attain to the quiet triumph of true resignation, which at the hour of its greatest need it can achieve over the circumstances of life.

We have seen then that if thought goes deep enough, it does bring us to an attitude of world- and life-affirmation. Now we must see if it will lead us to any conclusions in the realm of ethics.

The basic principles of morality hitherto set up are unsatisfying, for they cannot be thought out to a conclusion without leading to paradoxes or losing in ethical content. The thought of antiquity tried to understand the ethical as that which brings rational pleasure. But starting from this standpoint, it failed to succeed in arriving at an ethic of active self-devotion, and it ended in resignation.

Modern ethical thought is from the outset social-utilitarian, taking it for granted that the individual shall in every respect devote himself to the welfare of other individuals and the welfare of the community. But when modern thought endeavours to think out this ethic and give it a sure foundation, it is forced to most remarkable and most inconsistent conclusions, and finally it can only explain the ethic of self-devotion or altruism as being based primarily on a wonderfully developed herd-mentality.

A third attempt to understand ethics is to explain morality as a striving for the realization or perfecting of the individual self, but this explanation fails so to establish the basic principle of the moral as to give it a content which is ethically satisfying.

45

The classical explanation of ethics is so obviously unsatisfactory that we need no longer consider it. There remain then these two contrasted attempts at explanation, the one starting from self-devotion as the recognized content of ethics, whilst the other starts from the self-perfecting of the individual, and tries to understand self-devotion as a necessary constituent of its content.

But is it not possible that self-devotion and self-perfecting, altruism on the one hand, and self-fulfilment on the other, belong together in such a way that the one is the corollary of the other? If we can combine the two ideas, we shall secure the true basic principle of morality. The first step towards success in combining them is to arrive at an understanding of why this process has not already been achieved.

In so far as regards the ethic of self-devotion, or helpful service to others, the fault must somehow lie in the fact that it has hitherto been too narrow. Social utilitarianism has been concerned on principle only with the devotion of man to man and to human society. The ethic of self-fulfilment on the contrary is universal, since it is concerned with the relation of man to the whole of creation. If then these two forms of ethic are to unite in one, the ethic of self-devotion must also become universal, and devotion must be directed not only towards man and society, but also towards all the manifestations of life upon this earth. But so far, not even the first step in the direction of universalizing the aim of devotion has been taken.

Just as the housewife who has scrubbed the parlour is careful to shut the door to prevent the dog from coming in to mess up the floor with his muddy paws, so do European thinkers take good care that no animals run about in the fields of their ethics. The stupidities of which they are guilty in their endeavour to maintain their traditional narrow-mindedness are, says Schweitzer, almost incredible. "It is as if Descartes, with his saying that animals are only machines, had bewitched the whole of European philosophy." Kant, to give but one example, specially emphasizes that ethics are concerned only with the duty of man to man. Whereas the thought of ancient India and ancient China, quite independently of each other, made ethics consist in kindly relations to all creatures. Take for instance the Buddhist saying, "As long as living creatures suffer, there is no possibility of joy for those who are full of compassion".[1]

The ethic of self-devotion must attain to the thought that it is concerned not only with mankind, but with every living creature, for "ethics are boundless in their domain and limitless in their demands". It must rise to the conception that the relation of man to man is only one expression of the relation in which man stands to Being and to the world in general. Thus universalized, or as Schweitzer puts it "become cosmic", the ethic of altruism can hope to meet and become one with the ethic of self-fulfilment, which is fundamentally universal or "cosmic" in character. In other words, each of us has to endeavour not only to maintain his own life at the highest possible level by becoming more perfect in spirit, but also has to endeavour to maintain other life at its highest level by sympathetic helpful self-devotion to

[1] Quoted in *Indian Thought and its Development*, p. 125.

it. What we call love is in its essence reverence for life.[1]

"But as soon as we in any way recognize the principle of love, even if we limit it to human beings, we arrive actually at an ethic of boundless responsibilities and duties. Love cannot be put under a system of rules and regulations. It issues absolute commands. Each of us must subjectively reach a decision for himself as to how far he can go towards carrying out the boundless commandment of love without surrendering his own existence. . . ."[2]

All philosophy, every world-view which can satisfy thought, must, as we have already shown, lead to mysticism. It must seek to give to human life such a meaning as will prevent man from being satisfied with being a part or manifestation of infinite Being in merely natural or physical fashion, and create in him through an act of consciousness the will to belong to this infinite Being inwardly and spiritually as well. In that union he can find strength in endurance and joy in action. The natural tendency of man's thought and the knowledge by which he recognizes his own being in the universal Being is in itself of a mystical nature. Nevertheless rational thought has hitherto called a halt whenever it approached the sphere of mysticism, whilst mysticism in turn has depreciated the value of reason, in order to elude any possible obligation to render a reasoned account of itself. Yet mysticism and reason belong together, because

[1] *Indian Thought and its Development*, p. 260.
[2] "Philosophy and the Movement for the Protection of Animals", by Albert Schweitzer, in *The International Journal of Animal Protection* (Edinburgh, May 1936).

if rational thought is pursued to its last conclusion, it must in the end lead to mysticism. Aristotle rightly declared that the beginning of all thought is wonder, for indeed thought loses all vitality when the sense of mystery is wanting. All profound philosophy, as all profound religion, is in the long run a striving after ethical mysticism or mystical ethics.

In the West our great mistake has been that we have imagined that without mysticism we can attain to a comprehensive philosophy of life capable of satisfying thought, and that is why European thought makes men moral but superficial, without inner personality or any realization of the need for it. The question what we shall make of our lives is not solved when we are driven out into the world with an impulse to activity, but with no power of reflection. It is an ethical question which can be answered only by a world-view which brings man into spiritual, inward relationship to other life. So we must give up abstract mysticism, and turn to the mysticism which is actively alive—a mysticism of action.

Now in philosophy all expressions such as the Totality of Being, the Absolute, the World Spirit, which are convenient to use, denote nothing actual, but only something conceived in abstractions. The only reality is the Being which manifests itself in phenomena, in the existence of individual beings. Totality of Being is an abstract concept, but infinite Being in infinite manifestations is an actuality. Again, it is only through the living manifestations of Being, and only through those manifestations with which we enter into relation, that our own individual being has any intercourse with infinite Being. The

4

devotion of our being to infinite Being is the dedication of our being to all living manifestations of Being which need our devotion and to which we are in fact able to devote ourselves. By this spiritual devotion we give meaning and richness to our own poor limited existences. In the mysticism of actual reality devotion is not merely a purely intellectual act, but an act in which the whole life of the individual has its share. There rules in it a spirituality which in itself both embraces and justifies our normal impulse to action. Ethics then is seen both subjectively and objectively as a limitless responsibility for all life that comes within the range of human life. It originates in the philosophy of world- and life-affirmation, and its basic principle is devotion to life out of reverence for life.

Reverence for life means forming a part of the infinite, unfathomable Will in which all being has its origin, and makes possible the realization of the idea of spiritual union with the Infinite through action. All living piety flows from it and from the compulsion to ideals that is given with it—piety which springs from an inner compulsion and asks no questions about the ends to be pursued. The will-to-live in profound reverence for life does not depend on personal happiness and success, but, because such a personal will-to-live thereby gains its own freedom from the world, gives value even to an existence which no longer seems worth living. In order truly to live, we must above all preserve our freedom.

If we let known facts tell us quite simply what is known about life, they will tell us that in and behind every kind of living phenomenon there is will-to-live. Progress in biological science consists only in increasingly exact de-

scription of the manifold phenomena of life, the discovery
of life where we previously failed to recognize it, and
the giving us the ability to adapt this knowledge to our
own uses. But no science can tell us what life is.

We do not know the nature of the various phenomena
of life, but we form a conception of their nature in
analogy with the will-to-live which is in ourselves. Thus
our knowledge of the world becomes part of our experience of the world and compels us to an inner relationship
with all life in the world. It fills us with reverence for the
mysterious will-to-live which is in all things.

True philosophy then must start from the most immediate and most comprehensive fact of consciousness,
and this, as we have seen, says: "I am life that wills to live,
in the midst of life which wills to live". This is a living
philosophy which can deal with all the facts of being.
A mysticism of ethical union with Being grows out of it.

As there is longing in my will-to-live for a continuance
of life and for the mysterious enhancement of the will-to-
live which we call pleasure, and as at the same time there
is a dread of annihilation and of the mysterious deprecia-
tion of the will-to-live which we call pain, so also with
the will-to-live that is all around us, whether it can express itself or not. A true system of ethics consists therefore in our recognizing and experiencing a compulsion
to show to all forms of life and of the will-to-live the
same reverence as that which we feel for our own life.

Here then is the basic principle of a new moral theory
raised to the level of a necessity of thought, namely: that
it is good to maintain and further life, and that it is bad
to destroy and thwart life. This underlies everything in

the ordinary ethical valuation of the relations of human beings to each other, since all moral obligations of one man to another can be described in terms of the maintenance or enhancement of life, material or spiritual, along with the effort to raise life to its highest value.

The basic principle of this morality demands not only a rearranging and deepening, but a widening of the current views of good and evil. A man is truly moral only when he recognizes and obeys the obligation always to give aid when possible to all life, and shrinks from wantonly injuring anything that lives. He does not ask in how far this life or that is valuable, nor whether it is capable of feeling. Life is sacred to him as such. He tears no leaf wantonly from a tree, wantonly plucks no flower, treads on no insect. If he sees a worm on the pavement after a shower of rain, he reflects that it will be dried up by the sun, if it is unable to burrow, so whenever possible he puts it on the grass alongside. If an insect is drowning in a puddle, he will hold a leaf or a blade of grass to help it to save its life. He is not afraid of being laughed at as sentimental. Every new truth is a subject for laughter before it is recognized. At one time it was regarded as laughable to assume that black men were really men and should be treated as men; and indeed over large areas of Africa they are still held by their white masters to be less than human. The time will come when people will be amazed that man needed so long a time to learn to regard deliberate exploitation of, or thoughtless injury to, not only man, but any form of life, as incompatible with true morality.

When the idea of reverence for life has once taken

possession of a man's thought, it never lets him go. Sympathy, love and all that is valuable in enthusiasm are comprised in it. In the mind it has gripped it works with unceasing vitality, involving it in the unrest of a ceaseless sense of unlimited responsibility. The question of success does not come into consideration at all. What will be significant for the world is the fact that in the ethically developed man there will have appeared a will-to-live filled with reverence for life and a self-dedication to all other life. After all, this is only an expansion of the sympathy with and service to other human life to which nature compels us. Our life originates in other life, and other lives originate from our lives and need our help to go on living. Ethics begins between members of the family, and must spread in widening circles till not only the family and the tribe, not only the nation, but all humanity, and not only all humanity, but finally all living creatures are included.

As an additional argument for the ethic of reverence for life, Dr. Schweitzer has of late years stressed the solidarity apparent in and between various forms of life, pointing to the fact that in animals also traces at least of ethical instinct and ethical conduct are discernible.[1]

"The physiological fact that our life derives from other life and other life proceeds from our life has a conspicuously spiritual significance. Primitive ethics arises from

[1] Cf. "The primary instincts that each individual brings with him are twofold; one set of instincts seeks his own preservation and welfare; the other takes satisfaction in the welfare of others. We call them egoism and altruism, self-interest and sympathy. Such instincts are innate, not alone in human nature, but in animal nature generally" (Viscount Samuel, *Belief and Action*, chap. ix).

the natural solidarity of man with his ancestors and descendants. But when man becomes a thinking being, the circle of his 'relations' grows wider. . . . So ethics derives from a physiological fact. The ethical is everywhere present in its beginnings, where there is a developed form of life which has to preserve life which has issued from itself."[1]

So wherever, for example, we find love and sacrificial care of parent creatures for their offspring, we may see the working of ethical power. There are instances also, which anyone much in sympathy with animals can recall, of them giving aid to one another. Schweitzer gives three examples, of which the first is as follows:

"It happened in a park (in Scotland) where a flock of wild geese had settled to rest on a pond. One of the flock had been captured by a gardener, who had clipped its wings before releasing it. When the geese started to resume their flight, this one tried frantically, but vainly, to lift itself into the air. The others, observing his struggles, flew about in obvious efforts to encourage him; but it was no use. Thereupon, the entire flock settled back on the pond and waited, even though the urge to go was strong within them. For several days they waited until the damaged feathers had grown sufficiently to permit the goose to fly. Meanwhile, the unethical gardener, having been converted by the ethical geese, gladly watched them as they finally rose together, and all resumed their long flight."[2]

We witness a horrible drama of the will-to-live divided against itself, of one existence supporting itself at the cost

[1] From report of Gifford Lecture in *The Scotsman*, November 12th, 1935.
[2] *Christendom* (Winter, 1936), p. 238.

of another, and it remains a painful enigma that we must live in a world dominated by creative will which is destructive and destructive will which is creative. The only light in the darkness is the fact that in us the will-to-live has become conscious of the will-to-live in others, and does manifest itself as desirous to become one with other will-to-live. Whenever my life devotes itself to other life, my will-to-live in fact experiences union with the infinite Will in which all life is one. My destiny therefore is to obey this higher revelation of the will-to-live. Knowing the one thing needful, I can disregard the inexplicable riddle of the world and of my existence. For in deepened devotion to his own will-to-live man does experience inward freedom from outward occurrences, and thus is able to devote himself profoundly and steadily to other life. This leads to that truthfulness towards oneself which Kant makes the very centre of his ethics. For example, ethics hitherto has held that one forgives another because one feels pity for him. But on these lines he who forgives feels he is tremendously good, and the other suffers humiliation. Reverence for life on the other hand, by reason of its essential union with other life, compels consideration for others and compels forgiveness for the sake of sincerity towards oneself. For the one knows he may be just as guilty as the other. Because I so often tell lies, I must forgive falsehood in others towards myself. Because I have been guilty of want of love, guilty of slander, deceit and arrogance I must forgive these faults when I am the victim. And I must forgive quickly, without drawing any attention to the fact. Indeed, I shall not actually forgive at all, for I shall not have reached the point of judging that there is anything to forgive. We have to carry on the war against evil by judging ourselves, not by judging others. Nor is it simply out of kindness to others that one must be gentle, peace-loving, forbearing and friendly, but from the need to be true to oneself, which is the most profound form of self-assertion.

But how does the ethic of reverence for life fare in the conflicts which arise between inward compulsion to altruism and necessary self-assertion?

Each of us is subject to the division of the will-to-live against itself. In a thousand ways our personal existence comes into conflict with that of others, and in the conflict we are compelled to destroy and to injure other life. In order to preserve our own existence, we have to defend ourselves against other existences which harm us. We are compelled to kill mice and slugs and insects of many kinds and to be mass-murderers of bacteria. We get our necessary food only by destroying plants and animals. And in this conflict our happiness is often built on injury necessarily done to our fellow-men.

Ordinary codes of ethics seek various compromises. But the ethic of reverence for life recognizes no relative obligations and condemns as absolute evil all destruction of life and all damage to life, whatever the circumstances. It does not allow us to let our feelings become blunted to any form of evil, for it abhors complacency. We are living in truth only when our conscious experience in our subjective ethical conflicts is constantly deepening, and even when we are obliged to take life or to damage life as a matter of necessity, it should be with compunction and with a bad conscience. "The good conscience", says Schweitzer, "is an invention of the devil."

When therefore we injure life, we must be quite certain that it is really necessary to do so, and we must never go beyond what is actually unavoidable. For instance, the farmer may rightly mow down a thousand flowers in his meadow when necessary in order to feed his cows, but he will be doing wrong if, on his homeward way, he wantonly knocks off the heads of flowers by the road-side by thoughtlessly flicking his stick.

"Those who experiment with operations or the use of drugs upon animals, or inoculate them with diseases, so as to be able to bring help to mankind with the results gained, must never lull any misgivings they feel with the general reflection that their cruel proceedings aim at a valuable result. They must first have considered in each individual case whether there is a real necessity to force upon any animal this sacrifice for the sake of mankind, and they must take the utmost care to ensure that the pain inflicted is made as small as possible. How much wrong is committed in scientific institutions through neglect of anaesthetics, which to save time or trouble are not administered! How much, too, through animals being subjected to torture merely to give to students a demonstration of perfectly understood phenomena. By the very fact that animals have been subjected to experiments, and have by their pain won such valuable results for suffering men, a new and special relation of solidarity has been established between them and us.

"From that springs for each one of us a compulsion to do to every animal all the good we possibly can. By helping an insect when it is in difficulties, I am attempting to cancel part of man's ever-increasing debt to the animal world. Whenever an animal is in any way forced into the service of man, every one of us must be concerned with the suffering which it has thereby to undergo. None of us must allow any suffering for which he himself is not responsible, if he can hinder it in any way, nor at the same time quiet his conscience with the reflection that by hindering it he would be mixing himself up in something which does not concern him. No one must shut his eyes and regard as non-existent the sufferings of which he spares himself the sight. Let no one regard as light the burden of his responsibility. While so much ill-treatment of animals goes on, while the moans of thirsty animals in railway trucks sound unheard, while so much brutality prevails in our slaughter-houses, while animals have to suffer in our kitchens painful death from unskilled hands, while animals have to endure intolerable treatment from heartless men, or are left to the cruel play of children, we all share the guilt.

"We are afraid of making ourselves conspicuous, if we let it be noticed how we feel for the sufferings which man brings upon the animals. We think at the same time that others have become more 'rational' than we are, and that they take as being usual and as a matter of course what we are excited about. Yet suddenly they will let slip a word which shows us that they too have not yet learnt to acquiesce. And now, though they are strangers, they are quite near to us. The mask in which we had misled one another falls off. We know now, from one another, that we are alike in being unable to escape from the gruesome proceedings that are taking place unceasingly around us. What a happy way of making a new acquaintance!

"The ethic of respect for life guards us against letting each other believe through our silence that we no longer experience what, as thinking men, we must experience. It prompts us to keep each other sensitive to what distresses us, and to talk and to act together without any feeling of shyness, just as the responsibility we feel moves us to talk and to act. It makes us keep on the look-out together for opportunities of bringing some sort of help to animals in order to make amends for the great misery which men inflict on them, and thus to step for a moment out of the incomprehensible horror of existence."[1]

Then again we are often obliged to discriminate between higher and lower forms of life, sacrificing the one to the other, but we must always remember that such discrimination is purely subjective and arbitrary, and does not imply that the lower form is worthless or unworthy of respect as life, or that we can rightly destroy it without compunction. The idea of there being any worthless life or any life which we may destroy and damage without compunction or regret is to be blamed more fundamentally than any other for the inhumanity of the present age.

"Anyone who has accustomed himself to regard the life of any living creature as worthless is in danger of arriving also at the idea of worthless human lives, the idea which is playing so disastrous a part in the thought of our time."[2]

Even in our relation to other human beings we are all tempted to lessen our guilt of inhumanity by with-

[1] *Civilization and Ethics*, pp. 256-258.
[2] Gifford Lectures. Report in *The Scotsman* of November 26th, 1935.

drawing as much as we can into ourselves, but such innocence is not honestly come by, and makes us resemble the housewife who leaves any killing to the cook. We must not shrink from responsibility. In every single case we must struggle to preserve our humane feeling, and it is better to err in favour of humanity than to act less humanely on behalf of some good aim that might be reached. All public activity is concerned not merely with facts that have to be realized in the interest of the community, but also with the forming of the opinions which are good for that community. This is more important than what is directly realized in the facts. He who, under the influence of a supra-personal sense of responsibility, when it seems advisable, simply sacrifices men and human happiness may accomplish something. But he has not done the highest and best thing possible, and his power is only external. We have spiritual influence only when men see that we do not frigidly decide things in accordance with principles laid down once and for all, but fight for our principle of humanity in every single case.

Moreover, each one of us has to decide for himself how much of his life, his possessions, his rights, his happiness, his time, his rest, his privacy he must sacrifice to others and how much he may keep for himself. Let no one judge another. The one thing that matters is that each shall value what he possesses as means to action, and whether this is accomplished by keeping and increasing possessions, or by giving them up, goes for nothing. What reverence for life commands has its own significance, even when it seems foolish and useless. It will not allow one fully to enjoy one's own happiness, but arouses disturbing thoughts of the misery of others. True ethics says, "You are happy, so you are called to give much. You must not take as a matter of course what you have received more than others in health, natural gifts, capacity, success, a happy childhood, harmonious home life. You must pay a price for these things." The voice of truth is dangerous for the happy, if they dare to listen to it. It tends to throw them out of their course and make of them those adventurers of self-devotion of which the world has all too few.

To those whose work leaves them little time or opportunity to devote themselves to their fellows, the ethic of reverence for life appeals to give some portion of their scanty leisure to the expression in one way or another of their humanity. What he has to sacrifice is each one's secret, but all of us must know that our existence only reaches its real value when we experience in ourselves something of the truth of the saying, "Whosoever shall lose his life, the same shall save it".

"Reverence for life demands therefore, as the ideal of the material and spiritual being of man, that, with the completest possible development of all his faculties and in the widest possible freedom, both material and spiritual, he should strive to be honest with himself and to take a sympathetic and helpful interest in all the life that is around him. In earnest concern about himself, he must ever keep in mind all the responsibilities which are his lot, and so, as sufferer and as actor, preserve in his relation to himself and to the world a living spirituality. There should ever be before him as true human nature the duty of being ethical in the profound world- and life-affirmation of reverence for life."[1]

In ethics we have to seek similar progress to that of the mariner when the magnetic needle was discovered which enabled him to know his position on the darkest night. As long as we had only a limited system of ethics, we directed our course by stars which, however brilliant, give only more or less reliable guidance and may be hidden by mist. During a stormy night they leave mankind, as we know by recent experience, in the lurch. But if we possess a universal system of ethics determined by a principle which is a necessity of thought, individuals will begin to reflect and the steady ethical progress of mankind will ensue.

There must come about a spiritualizing of the masses. Countless individuals must begin to think about their lives and aims. And although we know that the preservation of civilization depends before all on the release of the fountains of spiritual life that are within us, we shall nevertheless face with zeal our economic and social problems. The greatest possible material freedom for the greatest possible number of people is required by civilization, but it is only through the principle of reverence for life that we can reach the standards of economic justice about which we have to arrive at an understanding. We *must* get to this state of development, if we are to avoid material and spiritual ruin. All progress in invention, all progress in the control of the forces of nature, has a fatal end unless by progress on the spiritual side we retain the

[1] *Civilization and Ethics*, p. 274.

mastery over it. Intoxicated by material achievement, we forgot to see to the advance of the human spirit, with the result that it has become almost impossibly difficult to have faith in spiritual progress. But we must find the courage to force our way to such faith, and we can and shall attain to it, if reverence for life begins to work in our thoughts. The power of the elemental and living spirituality to be found in this conception is incalculable. Moreover, "only such thinking as brings power to the spirit of reverence for life is capable of bringing perpetual peace to mankind. . . ."[1]

[1] *Ibid.*, closing sentence.

Epilogue

"FOR there must indeed arise a philosophy profounder and more living than our own and endowed with greater spiritual and ethical force. In this terrible period through which mankind is passing, from the East and from the West we must all keep a look-out for the coming of this more perfect and more powerful form of thought, which will conquer the hearts of individuals and compel whole peoples to acknowledge its sway. It is for this that we must strive."—*Indian Thought and its Development*, p. x (1935).

Bibliography

I. *Books by Albert Schweitzer*

AFRICA

ON THE EDGE OF THE PRIMEVAL FOREST. 1922. London: A. & C. Black. Transl. C. T. Campion. Pp. 176. 10th impression 1937. New York: Macmillan.

Zwischen Wasser und Urwald. Bern: Paul Haupt. München: C. H. Beck. Pp. 154.

Also French, Swedish, Dutch, Danish, Finnish and other translations.

MORE FROM THE PRIMEVAL FOREST. 1931. A. & C. Black. Transl. C. T. Campion. Pp. 169. New York: Henry Holt ("The Forest Hospital at Lambaréné").

Mitteilungen aus Lambarene. Drei Hefte 1925, 1926, 1928. Bern: P. Haupt. München: Beck.

Also French, Swedish, Dutch translations.

FROM MY AFRICAN NOTEBOOK. 1938. London: Allen & Unwin. Transl. Mrs. C. E. B. Russell. Pp. 132.

Afrikanische Geschichten. 1938. Leipzig: Felix Meiner.

Afrikanische Jagdgeschichten. 1936. Strasbourg: Éditions des Sources. Pp. 16.

AUTOBIOGRAPHY

MEMOIRS OF CHILDHOOD AND YOUTH. 1924. London: Allen & Unwin. Transl. C. T. Campion. Pp. 103. New York: Macmillan.

Aus meiner Kindheit und Jugendzeit. 1923. München: C. H. Beck. Pp. 64.

Selbstdarstellung. 1929. Leipzig: Felix Meiner. Pp. 42.

MY LIFE AND THOUGHT. 1933. London: Allen & Unwin. Transl. C. T. Campion. Pp. 283. New York: Henry Holt ("Out of My Life and Thought").

Aus meinem Leben und Denken. 1932. Leipzig: Felix Meiner. Pp. 211.

MISCELLANEOUS

Eugène Münch. 1898. Mulhouse, Alsace: Brinkmann. (In French.)

Bibliography

Goethe Gedenkrede. 1932. München: C. H. Beck. Pp. 51. English translation published in "The Hibbert Journal".

MUSIC

J. S. BACH. 1911. London: A. & C. Black. Transl. Ernest Newman. 2 vols. Pp. 428 + 500. 4th impression 1938. New York: Macmillan.

J. S. Bach, 1908. Leipzig: Breitkopf und Härtel. Pp. 828. 5th edition 1922.

J. S. Bach, le musicien-poète. 1905. Paris: Costallat. Pp. 455. 4th edition 1924.

Deutsche und französische Orgelbaukunst und Orgelkunst. 1906. Leipzig: Breitkopf und Härtel. Pp. 51. 2nd edition with supplement, 1927.

J. S. Bachs Orgelwerke. Kritisch-praktische Ausgabe. Zusammen mit Charles Marie Widor. 1912–1914. New York: G. Schirmer. 4 vols.

Der runde Violinbogen. Separatabdruck aus Schweizerischer Musikzeitung. No. 6. 1933. Pp. 7.

PHILOSOPHY

Die Religionsphilosophie Kants. 1899. Freiburg i/B.: J. C. B. Mohr (Paul Siebeck). Pp. 325.

THE DECAY AND THE RESTORATION OF CIVILIZATION. 1923. London: A. & C. Black. Transl. C. T. Campion. Pp. 105. 2nd edition 1932. New York: Macmillan.

Kulturphilosophie I: Verfall und Wiederaufbau der Kultur. 1923. München: C. H. Beck.
Also Swedish, Danish, Dutch translations.

CIVILIZATION AND ETHICS. 1923. London: A. & C. Black. Transl. J. Naish. 2nd edition (revised) transl. C. T. Campion. 1929. Pp. 285. New York: Macmillan.

Kulturphilosophie II: Kultur und Ethik. 1923. München: C. H. Beck.

INDIAN THOUGHT AND ITS DEVELOPMENT. 1936. London: Hodder & Stoughton. Transl. Mrs. C. E. B. Russell. Pp. 265.

Die Weltanschauung der Indischen Denker. Mystic und Ethik. 1935. München: Beck. Pp. 195.

THEOLOGY

THE QUEST OF THE HISTORICAL JESUS. A Critical Study of its Progress from Reimarus to Wrede. 1910. London: A. & C. Black. Transl.

W. Montgomery. Pp. 401. 2nd edition 1911. Reprinted 1922, 1926. New York: Macmillan.

Von Reimarus zu Wrede. 1906. Tübingen: J. C. B. Mohr. Pp. 418.

Geschichte der Leben-Jesu-Forschung. Neu bearbeitete und vermehrte Auflage des Werkes *Von Reimarus zu Wrede.* 1906. Tübingen: Mohr. Pp. 642. 2nd edition 1913.

PAUL AND HIS INTERPRETERS. 1912. London: A. & C. Black. Transl. W. Montgomery. Pp. 249. New York: Macmillan.

Geschichte der paulinischen Forschung von der Reformation bis auf die Gegenwart. 1912. Tübingen: Mohr.

THE MYSTERY OF THE KINGDOM OF GOD. 1925. London: A. & C. Black. Transl. Walter Lowrie. Pp. 275. New York: Dodd, Mead.

Das Abendmahlsproblem. 1901. Tübingen: Mohr. Pp. 62. 2nd edition 1929.

Das Abendmahl. Zweites Heft: *Das Messianitäts- und Leidensgeheimnis.* 1901. Tübingen: Mohr. Pp. 109. 2nd edition 1929.

CHRISTIANITY AND THE RELIGIONS OF THE WORLD. 1923: Allen & Unwin. Transl. J. Powers. Pp. 86. New York: Doubleday, Doran.

Das Christentum und die Weltreligionen. 1924. Bern: Paul Haupt. Pp. 60. Also Swedish, Danish, Dutch and Japanese editions.

THE MYSTICISM OF PAUL THE APOSTLE. 1930. London: A. & C. Black. Transl. W. Montgomery and F. C. Burkitt. Pp. 406.

Die Mystik des Apostels Paulus. 1930. Tübingen: Mohr. Pp. 385.

Die psychiatrische Beurteilung Jesu. 1913. Tübingen: Mohr. Pp. 46.

II. *Some of Albert Schweitzer's articles in periodicals*

"Everyland", Vol. III (a children's annual: The Carey Press). *Our Pets at Lambaréné,* pp. 36-38, 88-90, 114-116, 150-151.

"The Contemporary Review", Jan. 1928. *The Relations of the White and Coloured Races.*

"The Hibbert Journal", July 1929, pp. 684-690. *On Goethe.* Transl. C. T. Campion. Reprinted as pamphlet by Henry Holt, New York.

"The Hibbert Journal", 1932. *The Goetherede.* Transl. C. T. Campion. Mutilated by editors.

"The Christian Century", March 18th, 1931, pp. 373-376. *Sunday at Lambaréné.*

"The Christian World", Nov. 1st, 1934, p. 11. Sermon on *Forgiveness.*

"The Animals' Magazine", Oct. 1935, pp. 3, 4. *Reverence for Life.*

Bibliography

"International Journal of Animal Protection" (Edinburgh), May 1936. In English and German. *Philosophy and the Movement for the Protection of Animals.*

"Christendom" (Chicago), Winter 1936, pp. 225-239. *The Ethics of Reverence for Life.*

French

"Europe" (Paris), Sept. 15th, 1927, pp. 61-88. *Premiers Mois à Lambaréné.*

"Revue des Deux Mondes", Sept. 15th, 1931, pp. 390-404. *Le Secours Médical aux Colonies.*

German

"Atlantis" (Berlin-Zürich), March 1932. *Nochmals Falkenjägerei.* Transl. "The Animals' Friend", Nov. 1932, pp. 319, 320.

Die Beziehungen zwischen den Weissen und Farbigen Rassen. 1931. A pamphlet printed privately. Largely quoted in "The Aryan Path" (Bombay), June 1932. *Practical Internationalism.* Mrs. C. E. B. Russell.

III. *A Few of the Innumerable Books and Articles about Albert Schweitzer*

C. T. Campion. *Albert Schweitzer: Some Biographical Notes.* 1928. London: A. & C. Black. Pp. 31.

Professor John D. Regester. *Albert Schweitzer, the Man and his Work.* 1931. New York: The Abingdon Press. Pp. 137.

C. F. Andrews. *What I Owe to Christ.* Chap XIII, "Albert Schweitzer". 1932. London: Hodder & Stoughton.

Mrs. C. E. B. Russell. *My Monkey Friends.* 1938. London: A. & C. Black. Pp. 126. Introduces Dr. Schweitzer to animal-lovers and young people. Temporarily out of print.

German

Oskar Kraus. *Albert Schweitzer, sein Werk und seine Weltanschauung.* 1925. Berlin: Pan-Verlag. Pp. 78. 2nd enlarged edition 1929. Kraus was Professor of Philosophy at the University of Prague.

Ernst Barthel. *Elsässische Geistesschicksale.* 1928. Heidelberg: Karl Winter, pp. 217-279, etc.

Karl Raab. *Albert Schweitzer, Persönlichkeit und Denken.* About 1938. Publisher anonymous. Pp. 95.

Martin Werner. *Das Weltanschauungsproblem bei Karl Barth und Albert Schweitzer*. 1924. München: Beck. Pp. 136.

Martin Werner. *Albert Schweitzer und das freie Christentum*. 1924. Zürich: Beer. Pp. 31.

Hans Wegmann. *Albert Schweitzer als Führer*. 1928. Zürich: Beer. Pp. 80.

Martin Strege. *Zum Sein in Gott durch Denken. Eine Darstellung der ethischen Mystik Albert Schweitzers*. 1937. Bern: P. Haupt. Pp. 106.

Dutch

Jan Eigenhuis. *Albert Schweitzer*. 1929. Haarlem: Tjeenk Willink. Pp. 260.

Swedish

Baroness Greta Lagerfelt and others. *Albert Schweitzer, Mannen och hans gärning*. 1938. Uppsala: J. A. Lindblad. Pp. 239.

In Periodicals

"The Manchester Guardian", May 10th, 1928, pp. 9 and 12.

"The Hibbert Journal", July 1925, pp. 695-708. W. Montgomery: *Schweitzer's Ethic*.

"The Hibbert Journal", July 1935, pp. 630-634. On *Indian Thought and its Development*.

"The Aryan Path", June 1935 (ditto), pp. 375-379. (Published Bombay. Many printers' errors.)

"The Aryan Path", June 1932, pp. 429-431. *Practical Internationalism*. Based on "Die Beziehungen zwischen den Weissen und Farbigen Rassen".

"The Animals' Friend", Nov. 1931, Jan., Feb., March 1933, March 1936, April 1936.

"Europe" (Paris), Sept. 15th, 1927, pp. 56-60.

"L'Illustré" (Lausanne), Feb. 14th, 1935, pp. 162-166.

"Revue Hebdomadaire" (Paris), May 22nd, 1937, pp. 409-423.

"Schweizer Illustrierte Zeitung", July 30th, 1930, pp. 1258-1265.

"Das Deutsche Buch" (Leipzig), 1928. Heft 11, 12, by Professor Oskar Kraus.

"Illustrierte Zeitung" (Leipzig), Dec. 8th, 1932, pp. 668, 669.

"Neue Freie Presse" (Vienna), Dec. 25th, 1932, by Stefan Zweig.

"Die Musik" (Berlin), Feb. 1931, pp. 334-337.

"Musik in Württemberg" No. 5, 1932, pp. 111-116.

"Die Medizinische Welt" (Berlin), Sonderabdruck nr 5. Pp. 8.